Deliver the
Package

Simple truths to help you set your genius free

For corporate employees

Stephanie Chick

Deliver the Package
Simple truths to help you set your genius free

Copyright © 2010 by Stephanie Chick

Deliver the Package and Delivery Tips are registered trademarks of
The Genius Group, LLC.

ISBN: 978-0-615-34701-1

Editing: Kellie Tabron, www.kellietabron.com
Copyediting: Hilary Achauer, www.hilaryachauer.com
Cover and Interior Design: Paul Durban, www.blazonfire.com

For further information: **www.deliverthepackage.com**

The truth **will** set you free.

For Gigi

This book of love and learning is your legacy.

The Contents

The Invitation

To Corporate Employees

You're invited to a place few seek, and even fewer find. It's a place where genius roams free.

This invitation is for:

- Women who want to flaunt their beauty, brawn, and brains.

- Men who are fed up with masking their pain.

- Baby boomers who are sick and tired and ready to find the exit door.

- Generation X and Y who are waiting in the wings, hungry to achieve more.

- Black people, Latinos, Asians, and Native Americans, too. Because packages come in all shapes, sizes, and hues.

If you can handle the truth, this book will teach you how to deliver the package. And the package will deliver *you*.

The truth is, there is a unique and special package inside of you. This package reflects who you really are and represents your true power and potential. The package is your **genius**. When you **Deliver the Package**, you unleash your genius and set it free. When you are free, you can achieve breakthrough success and boundless possibilities—at work and in life.

Every employee wants and deserves to be free. Free to express their individuality and authenticity; free to maximize their gifts and abilities; free to help their company succeed without compromising their own wants and needs. This book will help you set your genius free so that you can fulfill your true hopes and dreams in the workplace and beyond.

Tell the truth. While lying awake in bed at night, or maybe drifting off in the middle of one of those endless conference calls, have you felt that little inkling; a nudge from somewhere deep within that craved something *more*? Be honest. Do you feel that your life is all wrong and you can't figure out how to make it alright? Admit it. Have you attained some level of professional success, yet you're still missing personal fulfillment and happiness?

If you answered "yes" to these questions, your genius is trapped.

I understand...

that you want to figure out who you *really* are and what you *really* want to do;

that you're tired of politics and pretense;

that you simply want to find success and fulfillment.

I understand how you're feeling and what you're going through. Before becoming a coach, I was a corporate employee just like you.

For over 15 years, I worked in corporate America in various sales, marketing, and management positions—first at IBM and later at HP. While working for HP, I attained all of the external benchmarks of business success—a six-figure income, stock options, promotions, and other perks. On the outside, life was good. But on the inside, it just didn't feel *good enough*. Ironically, in the midst of achieving my highest professional goals, I found myself feeling completely unfulfilled deep within my soul.

For years, I ran from this truth—constantly seeking new job assignments, finding activities outside work to distract me, and using material success to mask the fact that my life was terribly off track.

Then one Friday afternoon, while working from home, I had a moment of truth. As I sat at my computer, a steady stream of tears trailing down my face, I suddenly realized that my running days were over. I was tired. Tired of doing what others expected of me, tired of playing it safe instead of pursuing my calling, tired of being afraid to unleash my true capabilities. It was time to face my fears and frustrations and figure out what I was really meant to do—professionally *and* personally. In that moment of clarity, I found conviction in this simple truth:

Life is short.

Something inside of me was yearning to be set free and I didn't want to spend the rest of my life settling and feeling unfulfilled and unhappy. That Friday afternoon I made a promise to myself. From that day forward, I would deliver *my* package instead of someone else's.

Step by step, I learned how to unleash my genius. Each day I became more confident and courageous and eventually, I gained clarity about the legacy I wanted to leave. I discovered that coaching was my calling and I changed my career direction inside HP. Finally, I had found a way to add value to my company without devaluing *me*. It was the most rewarding time of my corporate career!

Even though I had found my calling, and was reasonably satisfied and happy in my work, a year later I still felt something pulling at me from deep inside, something urging me to keep going. In 2006, I made the difficult choice to leave HP. I didn't leave because I was fed up and miserable with corporate life. I left simply because I needed to go wherever my genius wanted to take me.

Leaving corporate America was a very tough decision. It's hard to walk away from the comfort of what is known and leap into the fear and uncertainty of the unknown. It was particularly difficult to leave HP because the company had given so much to me—and I had given as much in return. It's hard to walk away from a relationship where you've invested so much—personal or otherwise. But I believe strongly in following your heart. The journey of unleashing your genius is about learning to trust yourself completely, even if it doesn't make sense to anyone else and scares the daylights out of you. To deliver your package, you have to learn to listen closely to what resonates deep within and stay grounded in your own truth.

After I left HP, I was fairly certain my days inside corporate America were done. But I soon found out that my genius had played a trick on me. Shortly after I left, I began to realize that I desperately wanted to return to help the employees I had left behind. I finally figured out what my genius knew all along—that I wanted to inspire and coach corporate employees everywhere, not just the ones at HP.

Let me be completely clear. **You don't have to leave corporate America to deliver your package.** While that happened to be the right decision for me, it's up to you to decide where to unleash your genius. You'll have to search *your* soul for the right decision, just like I did. Just remember that wherever you choose to unleash your potential, the prerequisites are the same:

- You must honor your values and stay focused on what matters most to you.

- You must fight your fears and forget about trying to please others.

- You must face the lies you've told yourself in order to find your truth.

Whether you're working in the trenches or in the top executive suites, staying true to yourself is the package we all want to deliver. Because life *is* short.

Deliver the Package shares the simple yet significant truths I learned during my journey to unleash my genius inside and outside corporate America. My hope for this book is that it inspires and motivates you to deliver *your* package and helps you discover how to make a living *and* have a meaningful life. I trust that the truths you learn here will be of lasting value while you're working inside corporate America—and that you'll take them with you if you ever choose to leave.

But for now, I simply invite you to sit back and relax in your favorite reading spot. Find a quiet place where you feel completely comfortable and at ease—a place where your genius can roam free.

This book is a gift of love and learning sent from me— special delivery to you.

Stephanie

Stephanie Chick

The Package

We all love to receive packages. Whether it's for Valentine's Day, a birthday, an anniversary, or just because, a package always brings a smile to our faces. A package also ignites feelings of excitement and anticipation—we can hardly wait to see what's inside.

When my brother Michael and I were kids we couldn't wait to open our Christmas packages. Michael told me that he had finally discovered who Santa's helper really was and that *she* would know exactly what Santa was bringing us. I had my doubts about this revelation, but it didn't stop me from going along with Michael's plan.

A few weeks before Christmas, Michael and I waited patiently for Mom to leave the house to run errands for a few hours. As soon as the car turned the corner, we scoured the house looking for the packages. We checked the closets in her bedroom, behind the couch in the living room, and downstairs in the basement. We looked in the garage and even desperately searched under our own beds. We looked all over the house, but we couldn't find the packages anywhere.

After several minutes of searching, I became tired and frustrated and was ready to quit. We hadn't found any of our presents and I was starting to get scared that Mom would return home at any minute and catch us. Michael pleaded with me to help him keep looking. He told me that we would only check one more place. I had lost interest, and just wanted to go back to my room and watch TV, but Michael kept bugging me. I reluctantly agreed to help him keep searching.

We had hurriedly checked Mom's closet once before and hadn't found anything. It was a long, narrow closet—very dark and *very* spooky, so the first time we looked in there we had searched quickly. We went back this time armed with a flashlight, and although we were frightened at what we might find, we slowly crawled back inside. At first, we still didn't find anything, but undaunted, we kept crawling, searching, and then suddenly ...

There ... in the back of the closet, behind winter coats and piles of shoes, we found a large shopping bag. We screamed and shouted because we knew we had finally found the loot! We dragged the bag from the back of the closet and poured the contents onto the bedroom floor. Inside we found Barbie dolls, G.I. Joe action figures, board games, and even the Easy-Bake Oven I had begged for. Michael and I were so happy and excited. We had found *everything* we asked Santa to bring us, and much more.

Of course, we quickly realized that we had ruined Christmas Day. But sometimes surprises simply aren't worth the wait!

That's the wonderful thing about a package. It doesn't matter if it's large or small. It can be delivered to you in person or left by the UPS driver at the front door. The package can be beautifully wrapped with a bow or it can come without any wrapping at all. No one cares about the size of the package, how it's delivered, or the way it's wrapped on the outside. The only thing we *really* care about is what's inside.

The Genius Within

Inside of you is a package eagerly waiting to be opened. The package contains your true power and potential—your **genius**. We all have a genius within. We all have unlimited gifts and abilities. We all have the power inside to determine our destiny.

You can rise from humble beginnings to become one of the most powerful people in the entertainment industry. You can run a billion dollar technology company before you reach the age of thirty. You can use your vision and your voice to change history. If you set your genius free, you can leave a lasting legacy in any area of your choosing.

You just have to believe. You have to believe that your power and potential are limitless. You have to believe that you can achieve improbable dreams. You have to believe there's a genius inside of you that can accomplish anything.

There are no limits to your success
if you believe you're a genius.

Unfortunately, the majority of the people I meet find it hard to believe they could be a genius. When I say to someone, "tell me about your genius," most of the time they immediately become uncomfortable. They often fall silent; not knowing exactly what to say. When I probe deeper, most people tell me that the reason they don't know how to respond is because the thought of being a genius is beyond their imagination.

The idea of being a genius seems elusive and unattainable because most people believe that only accomplished and revered people like Einstein or Mozart are geniuses. The common belief is that it takes notoriety or a Nobel Prize to be deemed a genius. Maybe a tech titan like Steve Jobs or a billionaire tycoon like Warren Buffet could be considered geniuses. But *me*, a **genius**? It couldn't be true.

> *It's easy to imagine being good at something,*
> *yet it can feel intimidating to think of being great.*

Remember this. When you fail to embrace your own personal greatness, you'll find yourself clinging to false beliefs. You'll think that somehow in life you drew the short straw. You'll feel that only people like Mother Theresa, Mandela, or Ghandi were born with genius in their genes. You'll wrongly believe that you are doomed to a life of marginal achievement and mediocrity. To deliver your package you must accept the truth that you, too, were born for greatness—and reject the lie that chance or circumstances have condemned you to a lesser life.

Genius exists within every employee—from individual contributors to C-level executives. There's a genius within every woman and man—from the youth of Generation Y to baby boomers on the brink of retirement. Regardless of your ethnicity, your educational background, or your life experiences, you possess *genius*. Every ordinary person has extraordinary potential. It just has to be set free.

There was a time in your life when being free wasn't so challenging ....

Genius is Child's Play

The best way to see genius at work is to watch children at play. Children approach life with spontaneity and a sense of adventure. Their spirits are open. Their voices are pure, raw, and uncensored. Their minds are full of wonder and curiosity. When my son, Eric, was in elementary school he wrote the following paragraph in his class journal about a day of discovery:

Yesterday I found an octopus in my bathtub. I would say, "Where on earth have you come from?" And he would say that he came from an ocean. Then I would say, "Let's go discover!" First we would go on a rocket. We would see Mars and see all of the aliens. Then we would watch Monday Night Football. Then we would see another octopus like the one I have. Then we would cook a barbeque. Then we would see a magic stone. Then we would go home.

Inside the mind and heart of a child, everything is possible. Genius roams free.

I was once sitting in the lobby of the doctor's office waiting for Eric to complete his school physical exam. While I waited, I was planning to reply to a few e-mail messages and browse through an outdated *People* magazine lying on a nearby table. But when a three-and-a-half-year-old genius named Camille walked in, I knew instantly that my plans would have to wait.

Camille walked boldly into the doctor's office. Her spirit was completely alive and uninhibited. She ran up to the reception desk, pulled herself up on the countertop, and leaned over to proudly point out the five stitches on her forehead to the office staff. I watched her twirl around in her beautiful print dress and she even played peek-a-boo with me.

Then she spotted a Lego table and immediately climbed down into the square hole in the middle. As she began crawling around on the floor, I asked, "What are you doing?" Without hesitating, she replied, "I'm in the ocean, swimming." When she came up for "air" she asked me if I liked the mountains on top of the table as she pointed to the yellow and green areas that framed the opening. I smiled and said, "Of course, I do."

Genius creates its own reality because
it's not confined by limiting beliefs.

After Camille grew tired of swimming she joined her mom and me on the couch. She was quiet for a few minutes—listening intently to everything we talked about. Then, suddenly, she announced that it was time to go to the bathroom and that she had to do more than pee. Her mother shook her head and I laughed out loud—amazed by how this child's spirit was so full of spontaneity and brutal honesty.

Watching Camille reminded me that we were all once this way. As children, we used to live in our own special world—a world of wonder and awe; a world where life was simple, straightforward, and *easy*. Unfortunately, we "grow up" and falsely believe that our approach to life and view of the world must change. But the truth is, the genius within wants things to remain the same—the same way it is in Camille's world.

No matter how old you are, your genius wants to play and to feel free. To your genius, a world of fantasy and fun is reality. The busy, boring world that adults get trapped in is only *make believe*.

The English biologist, Thomas Henry Huxley, said, "The secret of genius is to carry the spirit of childhood into maturity." That's exactly what Einstein did. In the biography, *Einstein*, Walter Issacson writes, "Throughout his life, Albert Einstein would retain the intuition and the awe of a child." The book also reveals that Einstein expressed the same sentiments about himself. In a letter to a friend, Einstein wrote, "People like you and me never grow old. We never cease to stand like curious children before the great mystery into which we were born." When you unleash the genius within, you recapture the boldness, bliss and boundless joy that reside in a child's heart.

Delivering your package is giving yourself
permission to rediscover who you used to be.

Stephanie Chick

The Loss

It's wonderful to see people who are curious, courageous and carefree. We watch their actions in awe because it's inspiring to see adults who still have the unbridled enthusiasm of their youth.

People like Richard Branson. He started a magazine in his teens, launched a record company in his twenties, and crossed the Atlantic in a hot air balloon in his thirties. And he plans to fly into space before he reaches the age of sixty.

Or the Archbishop Desmond Tutu. He hasn't lost that twinkle in his eye. On an episode of the Sundance Channel show "Iconoclasts," Richard Branson teaches Archbishop Tutu how to swim. It brought a smile to my face to see a 77-year-old man giggle and splash around in the water like he was eight.

Even a fictional person like Forrest Gump can teach us about courage and wonder. In the movie, Forrest only has an IQ of 75, but he's smart enough to follow his destiny. Through his eyes we learn to appreciate life's simplicity.

These are examples of people who carried the spirit of childhood with them as they matured. Instead of giving up their childish ways, they continued to imagine and believe. If your life isn't filled with magical moments and impossible dreams, your genius will go into hiding. And you'll lose out on having the life that was meant to be.

Life will be good but it won't be *great*.

You'll likely go about your day unaware and unfazed because ignorance *is* bliss.

Then one day you might notice that something has changed. On the inside you just don't feel the same. You're not as happy as you used to be. No matter what you do your soul isn't at peace. That undeniable uncomfortable feeling means that you've lost *you*. But on the outside you'll keep pretending it isn't true.

It puzzles me that people quickly call the
doctor when they have a common cold, yet
do nothing when sickness grips their soul.

Losing sight of your genius doesn't happen overnight. It happens over a number of years. It happens each time you settle for doing the things that you think you should. It happens every time you say, "Really, I would change things if I could." Genius goes into hiding whenever you stop seeking truth. When you ignore truth, life loses its sweetness and each day the good life slowly slips away. As you become more miserable and frustrated, you'll wonder ...*how did this happen to me?*

Life has gone from good to *hate*.

Many employees feel this way. Most just complain about how life "sucks" to family and friends. Some suffer in silence. Only a few are courageous enough to ask for help when the loss becomes too much to bear.

On the following page are excerpts from actual e-mail messages I've received from employees who finally realized they had lost their identity:

From a senior HR manager

I'm a 40-year old professional woman who is at a crossroads. I'm the mother of a young daughter and married to a great man. My career life is bottoming out from the fulfillment perspective. I am excited about [finding] my next career and living and working in my purpose. I am moving towards taking a self-declared "sabbatical" in the coming weeks/months in order to spend a little more time with my family but also to get some clarity about my next steps.

From a law clerk

To need my inner genius "delivered" is an understatement. As a matter fact, I could not sleep last night, because I just couldn't stop the volcano of "tears of not knowing how to be the best me" from falling.

From a marketing manager

I am sitting at my nice window seat at my "dream company"...surrounded by an amazing number of fun, kind and smart colleagues. For some reason, today is one of way too many days in a row now that I want to jump out my 3rd floor window to escape this job! I feel I've officially lost my package...and I'm desperate to do something I actually want to wake up for most mornings! Can you help me?

These messages reflect the yearning that many people have to deliver their packages. Their words reveal the *hidden* voice inside much of today's workforce—the frustrations and disappointments that come with untapped potential and unrealized dreams. Unfortunately, the voice of unmet desire can be found deep within the hearts and souls of far too many employees. This was certainly true for me. At one point during my corporate career, I became so lost and unhappy that it affected me both physically and emotionally.

While working at HP, I was on a flight from my home in San Diego, California to Boise, Idaho, to attend a planning meeting with my new marketing team. Midway through the flight, I started experiencing severe chest pains. I didn't know what was happening. At first, I thought that maybe it was just some minor indigestion or gas from something I ate. I hadn't packed any antacids, which I had started taking more frequently in recent weeks, so I tried drinking club soda and then ginger ale, but nothing offered relief. As time passed, I really started to worry. The pain got so bad that I began to wonder if something much more serious was wrong with me. I was only 39 years old, but was I having a heart attack? As the plane began its final descent, the pain became almost unbearable. I vacillated between pushing the flight attendant's call button for help and using the Airfone to say my final "goodbye" to my husband, Don.

But instead, I did nothing. That's right, nothing. I just sat there in a state of panic quietly praying to God to let me survive long enough to get off the plane and die alone in the Boise airport. I had even figured out the perfect place to perish—a bathroom in a very quiet area on the lower level near baggage claim. *Crazy*! What was even crazier is the reason why I didn't ask for help. One of my superstar employees was sitting a couple rows behind me. It had taken me a long time to recruit him to my team and I didn't want to do anything that would alarm *him*. Instead of asking for help, I sat in my aisle seat frozen in fear, trying to come to grips with the fact that this was how my life would end. Something was definitely wrong with me!

Well, clearly I didn't die in the Boise airport bathroom. A call to my doctor revealed that my "heart attack" was probably just an extreme case of acid reflux brought on by stress. But that frightening experience made it clear to me that my life was a mess!

On the return flight home, I felt exhausted and emotionally drained. By the time I got behind the wheel of my car and left the airport for the short drive home, I could barely see the road because I was crying uncontrollably. When I reached the cul-de-sac to my house, I stopped, pulled over, took out my cell phone and dialed my good friend, Linda. All I could say between the sobs was "My career ... my life ... I know this isn't it." She tried her best to console me but we both knew that no one could help me through this situation but *me*. I had to save myself from the life I was living.

After talking things over for a few minutes, I hung up, pulled my car into the driveway, and tried my best to compose myself. I walked into the house, went into the family room, and with a forced smile said hello to my husband and son. Neither said anything back. They just sat there, staring back at me blankly. In the silence I could see truth written all over their faces, because "dead woman walking" was written all over mine. I knew that I couldn't fake it anymore. I turned around and slowly walked upstairs to the bathroom in the master bedroom, turned on the lights, and looked in the mirror. I looked at my tear-stained face, my really bad hair day, and the harsh reality that my spirit had long since left my body. I called for my son. "Eric! Get the camera and come upstairs!" I wanted to capture the exact moment I knew for sure I was lost.

I know from direct experience what it's like to desire change and to *not* know where to begin. I know about feeling fearful and powerless. I know for sure what it's like to pretend. I also know that if you're feeling lost right now you didn't intend for things to turn out this way. You didn't mean to get off track. You didn't plan to lose sight of your genius.

Like me, you just took the wrong path...

Wrong Expectations

If you convince yourself that you can't have work/life balance, you'll always be stressed. If you believe you're powerless, you'll let others define your success and happiness. If you think it's okay to settle for being second best, your genius will stay trapped.

You always get what you expect.

To deliver your package you have to set the right expectations for yourself. You can't accept whatever happens to you. You can't let others define your truth.

Inside many companies, the "bell curve" is the barometer for success. Forced ranking may have you convinced that only a select few are capable of doing great things. This simply isn't true. **You** determine your destiny—not the powers that be. A client's story provides a great example of this fact.

Casondra was a sales administrative assistant. It was a job she liked a lot but it wasn't a job she *loved*. She took the job to get a foot in the door, but over time she realized that she wanted to contribute so much more. But instead of taking control over her life, she quietly did her job, never asked for what she wanted, and waited patiently for things to change. Before she knew it, two years had passed and things stayed the same.

Then one day Casondra decided she had waited long enough. At a staff outing, she was invited to give a brief presentation to the management team about her career goals. She knew this was her chance to share her true desires with her direct manager and other senior leaders. Although she was a bit nervous, she spoke confidently and honestly. Casondra talked about her previous experiences and the awards and recognition she had received. She spoke about wanting to add more value and play a larger role on the team. Most importantly, Casondra seized the moment to announce that she was going to compete for one of the newly announced sales rep openings.

Things don't change. People do.

Even though Casondra had previous sales experience and a proven track record of success, she faced an uphill battle to change jobs. Some people didn't think she was ready. Others didn't think she was worthy. They saw her solely as an administrative assistant. Despite the push back she persisted, and three months later she finally received an offer to join the sales team. Six months into her new role, she proved the naysayers wrong when her colleagues voted her the team's MVP!

When you are trying to deliver your package, people won't always be eager to support your goals or accept the changes they see in you. It can hurt when this happens, but you can't let it derail or destroy you. Remember that you have to view life through your own lens—not by someone else's limited perceptions. When others say don't—DO IT!

The loss of genius begins when you stop expecting more and start settling for less.

Wrong Environment

Another way to end up on the wrong path is to remain in the wrong environment. Your genius needs the right environment to flourish and grow. The right environment will allow you to reveal your uniqueness and authenticity. In the wrong environment, you'll conceal your true identity.

Shakespeare said, "All the world's a stage, and all the men and women merely players." On the corporate stage, many employees play their parts rather convincingly—smiling on the outside while sulking on the inside; nodding their heads yes when their hearts are really saying no. I know, because for years I gave an Oscar-worthy performance of my own—wearing a mask because I wasn't comfortable being me.

It wasn't a great place to be.

If you ever find yourself in an environment that stifles your self-expression and individuality, you have two choices. You can leave. Or you can change your beliefs. Often, it just takes a change in perspective to set your genius free.

When I first met Ed he told me that he never felt at ease in his work environment. He didn't have much trust in people. The people he trusted the least were "management." Ed was suspicious and skeptical of people in power because he didn't think *they* had his best interests in mind. He felt that if he took risks or shared his real opinions, it could jeopardize his career. Ed believed that the only way to succeed in the corporate environment was to play the game. So he played it safe and told management what he thought *they* wanted to hear.

Like many people, Ed was motivated by **fear**.

He was afraid to talk about his ideas and interests. He feared that senior leaders wouldn't really understand or honestly care about him. He believed that putting his trust in management would only lead to broken promises and disappointments. Ed's fears controlled his life, which made him overly self-conscious and constantly stressed. And because of stress he stopped working out and taking care of himself. He wasn't winning at the game and the game was beginning to impact his health.

That's when Ed finally realized that it was time to stop "gaming" and take a gamble on just being himself. He became more open and honest with his manager about his real wants and needs. He even initiated constructive conversations with senior leaders about what mattered most to him as a minority working inside a Fortune 500 company. To his surprise, people didn't reject him or his ideas. They welcomed his passion and fresh point of view. Over time, Ed regained his confidence and his colleagues were able to see the true leader that was hidden within. And a year later, *they* promoted him to management.

Sometimes your external environment is simply a reflection of what's going on inside of you.

The political game will always exist inside corporate America. But playing politics is not just about playing defense. Take the offense. Ask for what you want instead of posturing and pretending. You don't have to fear those who possess power and influence. The right work environment isn't win/lose—it's win/win. Always assume that others want what's best for you. Just remember that sometimes you'll have to teach others how to play by *your* rules.

But after you've done all that you can do you—if you still feel that the environment you're in isn't right for you... game over. Write your resignation letter and pack up your desk.

It's time to leave.

Wrong Experiences

Engaging in the wrong experiences will also keep you from finding the right path. Throughout most of my corporate career, my work experiences followed a typical pattern. When I got a new job, the first few months were exciting and stimulating. I'd work night and day, eager to learn and to grow. But after six months the newness would wear off, the challenge would be gone, and inevitably I'd become restless and bored. I'd search the Internet, go shopping over lunch, or take up a new hobby—anything to keep myself busy.

When you're always in the hunt it's
because you're hungry for more.

By the time I was hired by HP, my desires had dissipated. I once had dreams of becoming a senior VP or maybe one day running my own company. But I had stopped yearning for challenging opportunities. I was content with simply coming into the office each day with a positive attitude and doing what was expected of me. I was ready to settle into a comfortable and cozy work life with a decent salary, above-average performance evaluations, and the respect of my peers. Then one day Todd Cromwell showed up to lead our organization and his arrival changed my attitude and the trajectory of my career.

The first time I spoke to Todd was the day he scheduled brief introductory meetings with each of his new employees. Naively, I thought the meeting was about reviewing my accomplishments and plans for the upcoming year. While I chatted away, Todd simply listened. Little did I know that he was sizing me up to see if I was ready to take on a more challenging assignment.

A few weeks after that initial meeting, Todd asked to meet with me again. This time I had no idea what he wanted. He and my direct manager were seated when I entered the conference room. I tried to anticipate what my fate would be but I couldn't read the looks on their faces. As I sat down, Todd thanked me for all that I had achieved. He told me he was impressed with my performance and that he was glad to have me on the team. Then, without warning, Todd announced that he wanted to change my job responsibilities. He asked me to become a team leader and bring a breakthrough product to market. My gut reaction was, *"What is he thinking?"* I had only been with HP eight months. I couldn't understand why he wanted a rookie like me to lead a team of *experienced* employees.

As I sat at that conference room table, all I felt was shock and disbelief. After a few moments of silence, I said to Todd, "You do know that I've never done this job before?" He looked directly at me and replied, "If you want the job, it's yours." I asked for a day to think it over. I wanted to talk to a few close friends and family members to get their opinions. As I nervously shared my fears and concerns with my friend, Greg, he interrupted me and said, "This sounds like a great opportunity. What's the problem?"

The problem was that before I was hired by HP, I had been out of corporate America for nearly five years working for a nonprofit and a major university. I was still getting acclimated to being back in the corporate world. I also had no previous product marketing experience and I knew that failing could be the end of my career. Although I was scared to death, I knew Greg was right. This was an opportunity of a lifetime that I couldn't resist. Even though I knew for sure that I'd have to endure many long nights and lots of stress, I said, "Yes!"

Once I started in my new role, I quickly learned that Todd's leadership style was to throw you into the deep end. If you sank to the bottom, he would dive in to help. Otherwise, he would watch you flail around and gulp water until you learned how to swim. To be honest, there were many times that I seriously thought about quitting, but Todd's silent support sustained me. In his eyes, I could see that he had complete faith and confidence in my abilities.

The experience of someone believing in you
will far outweigh your fears and uncertainties.

I eventually succeeded in my role as a product manager and ended up working with Todd for six years. Each year he continued to give me even more challenging assignments that strengthened and stretched me. By the time I moved on to other organizations inside HP, my resume had grown tremendously—filled with rich and rewarding experiences in business development, e-business, and marketing. With Todd's support, I developed a proven track record and received many promotions and pay increases. I earned everything I got *and* I know that I owe a debt of gratitude to Todd for seeing potential in me.

Todd and I will be friends for life. I still call him every few months just to say hello. We talk about our families and rehash the same old stories. Before we hang up, I try to remember to tell him how much I love him and to thank him again for what he did for me. He awakened my genius by giving me experiences that were far outside my sight, yet well within my reach.

At times in your life you might take the wrong path—lingering too long in the wrong environments filled with the wrong expectations and experiences. It may take awhile to figure out the right direction and get back on track. Be patient.

Sometimes you have to get lost to find yourself.

Stephanie Chick

The Reasons

There's value in learning to be patient when you're lost and confused. Once you set off on the path to delivering your package, some days you'll know exactly which way to go and what to do. On other days, you'll have to sit still until the answers you seek are revealed to you.

Sometimes, you can't rush truth.

No matter how long it takes or how many obstacles or roadblocks you face, keep searching for your genius. Don't give up when the going gets tough. Don't become content and complacent and convince yourself that life is *good enough*. Keep searching even when you're full of doubt and uncertainty—even when you think you've exhausted all possibilities. When truth seems elusive, don't stop seeking. Do whatever it takes to find your genius and set it free!

There are two important reasons you must deliver your package: one is business; the other is personal. The business reason will make you rethink what it takes to succeed; the personal reason will force you to focus on the *right* priorities. Both reasons will stir your soul to action and coax your genius out of hiding.

The Business Reason—Talent Isn't Enough!

Talent isn't enough in today's business environment. Neither are your years of work experience, exemplary performance evaluations, or advanced degrees. Yesterday, the talented ones were recognized, rewarded, and retained inside companies.

Today, many talented people are out on the street.

The business world has become increasingly complex and competitive. As a result, the rules for success have been re-written. No longer can you rely solely on your skills and abilities to secure promotional opportunities or maintain your job security. You're poised for failure if you continue using yesterday's strategies. To survive and thrive in today's economy you need a different approach—a *new* and distinct strategy that will help you distinguish yourself among your colleagues and bring more value to your company. Now, more than ever, you must harness your genius because having talent is no longer enough to succeed.

Talent isn't enough because times are tough. As I finalize this manuscript, it's 2009 and we're in the middle of the worst recession since the Great Depression. Spending is down, credit is tight, and unemployment rates are skyrocketing. Companies and their employees are struggling. Even before the economic downturn, times were challenging. What drives today's business world is the insatiable demand for innovation, ingenuity, and speed. The companies that can consistently deliver a clear and compelling value proposition will rise to the top. The ones that *can't* will perish quickly because today's marketplace is impatient and unforgiving. The pace of change and the competitive forces at play are unprecedented. But you better get used to it because it's a new day! The recession will eventually end but *tough times* are here to stay.

To survive and thrive during these times, companies need more than talented employees. They need employees with inquisitive minds and ingenious ideas to lead their sales, finance, and business development teams. They need employees who can uncover growth areas and generate new income streams—a no-holds-barred type of employee who can develop breakthrough business models and implement bold marketing strategies. In good or bad times, companies need more than talented employees who can solve problems—they *want* creative geniuses who can see possibilities.

The Difference Between Talent and Genius

Your talents are your unique gifts and abilities—the things you're really good at and that come naturally to you. It could be your ability to analyze numbers, bring products to market, or deliver an inspiring presentation. Everyone has talent of some kind. But talent isn't genius. Genius is talent *unleashed*. It's the ability to take that talent and extend it beyond your core skills and strengths—unleashing your creativity and unlocking hidden capabilities. Your genius is the *latent* talent and potential that exists within you. Tapping into it will require a subtle yet significant shift in your thinking.

Talent creates. Genius innovates. Talent excels while genius exceeds. To quote the nineteenth century German philosopher

Arthur Schopenhauer, "Talent hits a target no one else can hit, while genius hits a target no one else can see."

Essentially, unleashing your genius is about being able to see things a bit differently. Einstein held a *different* view about space and time. Oprah created a billionaire-dollar empire by changing to a *different* talk show format. Google co-founders Larry Page and Sergey Brin figured out a *different* algorithm that produced a better search engine. Allow yourself to think differently and you, too, can achieve great things.

So why don't more people choose to think unconventionally? I believe it's because examining new perspectives leads you into unchartered territory. Innovative ideas, new theories, and breakthrough strategies will force you to let go of the status quo. It can be scary to venture into unfamiliar places on your own.

When I left HP and launched my own business, I was scared to death! I didn't have a long client list; I didn't know how I was going to keep my kid in private school; I was really afraid of failing and looking like a fool. But in order to unleash your genius you have to push your fears aside and step outside your comfort zone.

Talent is driven to master what is known.
Genius is marveled by the unknown.

It's also hard to break free and embrace new thinking if your spouse just got laid off, you're worried about how you're going to pay your mortgage, and you're up all night trying to figure out how you're going to meet your family's basic financial needs. It's tough to think about unleashing your genius when you're focused on keeping your nose down, not rocking the boat, and flying below the radar to keep your job security. The truth is hunkering down and running from your fears is never the right approach. No matter what state the economy is in, if you believe you have the power within to succeed, you will stay driven, determined, and undaunted.

> *Unleashing your genius gives*
> *you unwavering confidence.*

The Rewards of Unleashing Your Genius

Recently, I had a candid conversation with Debbie, a former client, who is a director at a major credit union. We talked about how her work life was different now that she had made the subtle shift from using her talents in the office to unleashing her genius. Debbie said, "When you focus on utilizing your talents you're always judging yourself against other people. You're never comfortable in your own skin. Now that my genius is unleashed I have much greater self-confidence." Instead of trying to measure herself against her colleagues, she trusts her own ideas and beliefs. The most significant change that Debbie has made since she unleashed her genius is honoring one important commitment every day. She said, "When I show up for work now, I *never* give my power away!"

Debbie admitted that reclaiming her genius hasn't always been easy. She learned that sometimes there's a price to pay when you dare to go your own way. Sometimes, when Debbie courageously shares new ideas at staff meetings her colleagues look at her strangely. When you see things differently people might think you're a bit crazy. It can be difficult to keep unleashing your genius when others don't understand your truth. You'll just have to be patient when people don't "get" you. Debbie said that she's learned to be more resilient and accept the potential consequences that come with having the courage to unleash her genius. No matter what the costs, she said she's going to stay the course.

> *The rewards of greater success and*
> *fulfillment are worth the risks.*

Having the courage to challenge conventional thinking is the hallmark of genius. It's only through bold moves that you'll find the next breakthrough. And when you do, sooner or later, the people that you work with will stop and take notice of you. Your manager and other leaders will be impressed and intrigued. Before you know it, you'll be the one that *everyone* wants to have on their team. When decisions are being made about the next workforce reductions or organizational restructuring, you won't have anything to worry about. Unleashing your genius will give you a competitive edge and boost your political clout. No matter what happens inside your company or with the economy, if you unleash your genius, you'll always be in high demand.

Talent can be escorted out the door.
Genius is never ignored.

The Personal Reason—Life is short.

Unleashing your genius will ensure that you stand out in a sea of talented employees and it will boost your business success. However, I know from personal experience and from coaching hundreds of corporate employees, that if your motivation for delivering your package is purely for professional reasons, you won't persist. It takes more than getting a promotion or a pay increase to keep you focused on setting your genius free. External rewards and recognition aren't enough to keep you in pursuit of unleashing your power and potential. You need a bigger reason to stay on the path to delivering your package.

What will motivate you to stay focused on *delivering* is remembering that time passes quickly. Think about it. One day you're a newly-minted trainee—then before you know it several years have gone by and you're months away from being a retiree. If you're not careful, in between that span of time, you'll lose your sense of urgency and forget all about your desires and dreams. Your life will be half over and you'll look up and suddenly realize that you've lived it cautiously, predictably... unremarkably.

That's why I made the choice to unleash my genius. I was nearly 40 years old and deep inside I knew that I hadn't begun to tap into my true potential. I had achieved professional success, but I hadn't found the courage to pursue *greatness*. As I sat crying in front of my computer on that Friday afternoon, I realized that I didn't want to waste another second settling for second best.

I remember a very truthful comment that one of my coaching clients shared with me. During one of our first coaching sessions, I asked her what she really wanted. Without hesitating, she said, "No regrets. I want to arrive at the end of my life regretting nothing." Her comments echo inside my head every day and remind me of why it's important to stay focused on setting your genius free. You don't want to find yourself at life's end wondering what could have been...

Each day you've only got 1,440 minutes available to you to focus on who you really are and what you really want to achieve—to find the courage to unleash your genius and follow your destiny. At the end of the day, those minutes will be gone. Kaput. History.

Unfortunately, many people fail to internalize this reality. One former client told me that she wanted to start her own nonprofit organization. The last time I spoke to her I asked her how her plans were going and she was silent. She was embarrassed to admit that she hadn't made any progress. Another person I met recently told me she wanted to become a C-level executive. When I asked her about what steps she had taken to achieve her goal she nervously said, "I haven't gotten around to securing sponsorship." It happens all the time. You hear people say I want *this*, I want *that*—and when you ask them about what they've done to achieve their goals, they tell you they're still looking into it. While they're thinking, waiting, and getting ready, the clock keeps ticking...

In a Fortune interview, Apple CEO Steve Jobs, said, "We don't get a chance to do that many things, and every one should be really excellent. Because this is our life. Life is brief, and then you die ... So it'd better be damn good." I think "damn good" is a far better way to approach life than settling for good enough.

Steve Jobs' candid comments are a sobering wake-up call for everyone, no matter who you are or where you work. Before you permanently put your true desires on the back shelf, remember that life is short. Don't shortchange yourself. The bottom line is—you've only got one life, one shot at success.

Don't spend your precious time
pursuing anything less than greatness.

Deliver the Package

Stephanie Chick

The Delivery Process

When you read a message and it resonates with you, the words leap off the page and capture your attention. You can instantly feel a profound inner shift when something meaningful piques your interest. That kind of resonance means that a message is significant to you—a clear sign that you've found *truth*.

If what you've read thus far rings true to you, and you have a strong sense that you're ready to unleash your genius, the Delivery Process will put you on the path to delivering your package.

The Delivery Process is a simple yet powerful process that will help you unlock your power and potential. It's a process that I use every day to help my coaching clients unleash their genius and it helps me to continue delivering my own package.

The Background

I discovered this process experientially—exploring, observing, and learning through trial and error. The day that I decided I wanted to set my genius free, all I had was will and determination. I didn't have a defined approach or a clear strategy. I simply surrendered to my soul and allowed my genius to guide me.

At the start of each day, I'd ask myself one simple question. *What next?* Then I'd sit quietly and listen closely for my genius to tell me the next steps to take—calling someone I had been afraid to approach, browsing around a gift shop after work looking for something intriguing, driving two hours out of town to take a screenwriting class just because it seemed interesting. Day by day, my genius guided me to opportunities, and with each courageous choice I began to discover what I truly wanted and desired. As I continued to make choices and take risks, my life started to change in positive and meaningful ways. I found my calling, the right people who could help me "magically" showed up just when I needed them, and I realized that I was beginning to feel more fulfilled and happy. Step by step, my desires and dreams were turning into reality.

As I continued to make progress, I became obsessed with figuring out the secret to my success. I wanted to know exactly what I had done that had helped liberate me. I wanted to understand how I went from wanting things to be different to actually taking steps to set my genius free. Day and night, as I'd get an insight, I'd jot down my thoughts in journals, on post-it notes, and on random scraps of paper. I didn't get the meaning of everything all at once. It was like working on a jigsaw puzzle. I had to focus on connecting the smaller pieces until I could see the bigger picture. Each day I searched for my truth relentlessly, and over time the process revealed itself to me.

The Roadmap to Reclaiming Your Genius

After years of chronicling my own experiences, I finally discerned that there were five key disciplines that helped me unleash my genius. These disciplines helped me tap into talents and strengths that I never knew existed inside of me—and opened up opportunities that I once thought were impossible to achieve. Each of these disciplines will also help you maximize your abilities and realize your dreams.

You must focus on all five disciplines every day—following just one or two won't suffice. Each discipline is an essential element of the Delivery Process and mastering all of them will be critical to your success in delivering your package. **Focus on five disciplines daily**—that's all you have to do to set your genius free. Don't think that solutions have to be overly complicated in order to be effective.

Simple acts often have the most profound impact.

Like with any disciplined activity, it takes consistency to reap results. The key to unleashing your genius will be your ability to stay engaged long after the initial excitement of trying something new has faded. That's where many of us fall short. For example, we make New Year's resolutions, and for a few days or weeks we stay on track. We get excited, feel great, and think we've got it made. But then work, family obligations, and other demands on our time sneak back in. We start making excuses and lose our focus and determination.

Unleashing your genius is a life-long journey. You have to be willing to "do the work" day after day, and learn how to find the magic in the mundane. To deliver your package, you have to keep exploring, discovering and learning ....

It is the quest, not the conquest, that unleashes genius.

The following five disciplines will help you unleash your genius. If you focus on these disciplines daily with courage and commitment, you'll maximize your success and fulfillment—at work and in life.

AWARENESS

To deliver your package you must first become aware of who you are—the distinct blend of values, passions, and strengths that define you. Maybe it's your artistic talent, your preference for working with numbers, or your insatiable interest in politics. Whatever unique combination of qualities you possess, you're unlike anyone else. The cornerstone to unleashing genius is understanding what makes you tick.

You can't realize your full potential
delivering someone else's package.

You're probably aware of who you are at a high level. However, to unleash your genius you must go below the surface—delving deeper and deeper until you discover your authenticity. Who are you at your core? What really drives and motivates you? Because, to quote German writer Johann von Goethe, "First and last, what is demanded of genius is love of truth."

There are many ways you can learn about your true self. Think about activities you like to participate in. What makes you feel excited and energized? When do you find yourself losing track of time? What do you do effortlessly? What are you doing when you're most at ease? You're delivering your package when you're involved in activities that come naturally to you and make you feel genuinely happy and at peace.

You can even learn about yourself by examining your home and work environments. Closely observe the objects that are lying around. Notice the ambience when you enter the room. What aspects of each environment reflect your real tastes and values? Is there something that's missing that has meaning or significance to you?

Or notice your reactions when you're having a conversation with a friend or a colleague. When do you lean in and listen more closely? When do you respond indifferently? What is said that makes you feel upset or angry? Your responses are simply a reflection of your real wants and needs.

No matter what you're doing, where you are, or who you're with, be more conscious. Being aware of your feelings and reactions in any situation can help you find clues to the real you.

Several years ago, my mother sent me a box filled with memorabilia from my early school days. The box had been stored away in her garage for years, but now she needed to clear out some stuff in preparation for moving to a smaller house. She sent the box to me for safekeeping and to make room for her own things. When the box arrived, I couldn't wait to open it. Inside I found academic and athletic awards; stacks of report cards dating back to kindergarten; a frayed and faded program from my first school play. I also found an inspiring letter from my favorite band teacher; a short story I wrote in fourth grade about a trip to the library; a handwritten draft of my high school graduation speech. Each of these items brought back fond memories of a time in my life when I was certain of who I was, and the things that made me happy. As I pored over the contents, an essay I had written for a college scholarship application caught my eye. As I read it and reminisced, I found myself drawn to one particular sentence that summarized my life's ambition.

> *By not limiting myself, I can continue to*
> *put the pieces of the person together*
> *and one day reach self-actualization.*

When I first read those words I laughed and said to myself, "What kind of 17-year-old kid talks like that?" Those words were deep for someone who still wore braces on her teeth and had to be home before midnight to beat curfew. But as I read the sentence a second time I suddenly thought, "This is **me!**" From deep inside I realized that those words reflected what I truly valued. I was surprised to discover that my passion for maximizing potential had been brewing inside of me for so long. I couldn't believe that as a teenager I already knew what was really important to me. I was amazed that while taking a trip back into time, unexpectedly, I found a clue to my identity.

You can gain awareness about yourself anywhere—sitting in a staff meeting, standing in the checkout line at the grocery store, or while spending quality time at home with your family.

If you stay curious and alert, everyday activities and situations will provide endless opportunities for self-discovery.

You'll find your truth if you keep looking.

Don't Keep "You" A Secret

Once you've gained awareness about who you are, go out and tell others. When you're able to speak openly and honestly with someone else about who you are it's a sign that you've fully embraced *yourself*. To unleash your genius you must be comfortable in your own skin. You must be willing to let down your guard and allow others to see your true essence. I'll admit that it's not easy to peel back the layers and reveal your true identity. But your genius doesn't want to be kept in hiding—it wants to be seen.

I remember one particular Friday morning when I found the courage to let others see the real me. I was at a networking breakfast meeting near my home in San Diego. After the keynote presenter finished speaking, everyone was asked to stand and briefly introduce themselves. I immediately cringed. I was less than excited about reciting my well-rehearsed and predictable elevator pitch, "Hi, my name is Stephanie Chick, and this is what I *do*." For some reason, on this particular morning, I felt compelled to tell the people in the room a much deeper truth.

But just before it was my turn to introduce myself, I started to feel nervous and *self-conscious*. A million questions were running through my mind. What would people think if I was completely open and honest? How would they respond? Would it be worth the risk? Up to this point, I had only spoken this truth within close, intimate circles—around people I felt totally safe and comfortable with. It's one thing to be truthful with your friends, family members, and close colleagues. They know and respect you. It's another thing to be forthright in a room full of complete strangers who could easily judge and criticize you. For a brief moment, I resigned myself to doing what was expected, but then I felt an unexpected surge of confidence. I suddenly realized that I had played safe for far too long. Enough was enough! The moderator pointed to me, I stood up confidently and said, matter-of-factly, "Good morning everyone. My name is Stephanie and I am a *genius*."

The room immediately fell completely silent. I looked around at the faces in the audience. Some were perplexed. Others looked surprised. A woman sitting at the table next to me had tears in her eyes. As I started to explain what I meant by my comments, the room erupted into spontaneous applause and cheers—and suddenly I was the one holding back tears. The crowd's response blew me away. I didn't know what reaction to expect, but I certainly didn't anticipate such genuine warmth and acceptance. During those anxious moments before I stood up to speak, I worried that people would interpret my statement as an extreme display of ego. Instead, the audience understood that I was simply voicing who I was, and what I knew to be true deep within my soul.

You take a risk every time you're courageous enough to be authentic. You could be judged, you might strain relationships, and you may even jeopardize your career prospects. Everyone won't always be accepting of you, but you can't look outside yourself for truth. Ralph Waldo Emerson said, "The difference between talent and genius is in the direction of the current: in genius it is from within outward; in talent from without inward."

Always follow your internal compass. Stay true to who you are. Do what feels right for you. You'll begin to unleash your genius when you learn to trust the voice within instead of being guided by external influences.

ATTENTION

Once you understand who you are, then focus on what you *really* want to do. Stop focusing on what you think you should be doing. Let go of meaningless activities that suck up your time and make room for what really matters most to you. If you keep trying to please others and continue doing things that diminish your spirit and drain your energy, you'll never get around to living your own dreams.

You have a calling. Your genius knows that there is something significant that you're supposed to do with your life. Your calling could be to develop the next killer app that transforms your industry. Perhaps your current position is preparing you to run a Fortune 500 company. Or maybe you'll make an impact by mentoring disadvantaged youth in your local community. You have a distinct purpose and you've got to figure out what "it" is. Keep your attention on finding and fulfilling your destiny. When your attention is focused on leaving a legacy your genius comes alive and your soul feels at peace.

Finding "It"

I'm often asked by my clients how I figured out that coaching was "it" for me. There's no magic formula for finding purpose. You just have to keep searching until you find the one thing that makes your heart sing.

I searched for my calling everywhere. I left corporate America for awhile to work for a nonprofit. I traveled alone to Mexico to study Spanish. I even took courses to become a massage therapist. I pursued anything and everything that piqued my curiosity, knowing that one day I would find "it" and me.

I've worked with so many people who try to "theorize" about what they want to achieve. They spend endless hours thinking about what could be, but very little time is invested in exploring possibilities. When you immerse yourself in testing and trying things out you'll figure out what you're called to do.

It's only through direct experience
that you can discover truth.

That's exactly how I found out that coaching was my calling—by attending an introductory class at a Marriott hotel in Pasadena, California on a summer weekend in June.

My friend, Heather, encouraged me to consider coaching because she said I had helped her so much throughout her corporate career. She told me that I seemed to really enjoy helping people succeed—and that maybe coaching could be the path to realizing my own hopes and dreams. I wasn't immediately sold on the idea... but I was somewhat intrigued.

For several months, I thought about what Heather said. Each time I recalled our conversation I could feel myself getting more and more interested, but every time I thought about giving coaching a try I hesitated. I avoided doing research to find the best coach training programs. I wouldn't tell my husband that I wanted to consider another career path. I rationalized that now wasn't the right time because my life was already too hectic. For some reason, I was afraid to take the first step.

The first step is always the hardest to take because you don't know what to expect. Trying to anticipate what will happen when you go from "here" to "there" can make you feel anxious and scared. When you don't know what lies ahead it sometimes feels safer to simply stay where you are and wait. But if you wait too long you could find yourself trapped in a never-ending battle between fear and faith. Just remember. Every courageous act brings you one step closer to discovering your destiny. As long as you keep moving, you will unleash your genius and find your calling.

That's why I finally signed up for my first coach training class. I knew I was stalling and making excuses. One day I really got annoyed with myself and finally decided to go for it. After all, the worst thing that could happen is that I'd find out that I didn't like it. Then I could move on to pursuing something else.

On the morning of the first day of class, I was asked to come to the front of the room to take part in a coaching demonstration. I was extremely nervous. When I walked to the front of the room my legs were a little shaky, but I was ready to face whatever challenge was waiting there for me. The instructor told me that she wanted me to help a fellow student discover what really made her happy. She told me to be curious and ask whatever questions came to mind. At first I was too worried about trying not to embarrass myself that I couldn't think of any questions to ask.

After a few terrifying minutes, I forgot about me and started focusing on the other person's interests and needs. Once I became engrossed in our one-on-one conversation, the questions started to flow freely. As I continued to listen to my "client" talk about the things that she was passionate about, I could feel my toes wiggling. I've learned that when my toes wiggle it's a sign that I'm headed in the right direction—an indication that I'm on the right path to delivering my package.

Your body is your built-in GPS. It will let you know when you're on track. It will also alert you if you're about to take a step that could sabotage your success or happiness. Pay close attention to your body's signals—the subtle, nuanced way that your body communicates to you. The tightness you feel in the top of your shoulders, the slight quiver in your gut, or the tingling sensation you feel in your toes. Every bodily sensation is a clue. You just have to stop and focus your attention to figure out what your body is trying to tell you. If you listen to your body's guidance every day, you'll rarely lose your way.

By the end of the weekend training class, I was beyond excited. I knew for sure I had found "it." After returning home, I spent the following week telling family members and friends, and anyone else who would listen, about my incredible experience. Since that weekend in June, many years ago, I have been fixated on one single goal—helping people unleash their full potential. I spend every waking hour consumed by this purpose because I know for sure this is what I am meant to do.

Talent is what you possess;
genius is what possesses you.
– Malcolm Cowley –

Holding the Focus

After you've found "it," your biggest challenge will be holding your focus on your goals and objectives. It can be hard to keep your eyes on the prize and not let distractions get in your way. The reason why it can be challenging to maintain your focus is because there is always something vying for your attention. At work, it's the constant chime of e-mail, the phone ringing, and the endless team meetings. Outside the office, you've got volunteer commitments and you have to deal with the demands of raising a family. When so many things require your time and attention, it's a daunting task to stay focused on your own priorities.

To deliver your package, you must be ruthless in guarding, nurturing, and protecting your dreams. No one else can or will do it for you. You'll have to become astute at sifting through and prioritizing what's most important, consciously choosing what you want to give your attention to at any given moment. At times, you will have to learn to say "No" or else you'll risk marginalizing your goals.

Without a steady mind and spirit, you'll find yourself enticed by every novel idea or opportunity you receive. Before you know it, your days will be mired in activities void of meaning and utility. In the midst of everyday chaos and constant choice, keep your attention on your intentions.

The essence of genius is to know what to overlook.
– William James –

ACTION

Once you have a clear goal or even an idea of where you want to go, take action. After you've determined your target, don't delay—go after *it*! Through action you'll continue to learn and grow—and the power and potential you possess within will continue to unfold.

Many people think this action needs to be something grand like quitting your job to pursue an advanced degree or dipping into your retirement savings to start a business. Not at all. To begin only takes one small step. Do some Internet research on your goal, take a class at night or on the weekend, or talk to someone who does what you'd like to do to learn more about their experiences. Take one small step each day and don't worry about what lies ahead.

Each step will lead to the next.

Trust Your Sixth Sense

Many people I've coached rely too heavily on reason and rigorous thinking to succeed. They expend all their mental energy assessing options and opportunities, believing that if they think on "it" long enough they'll figure out how to proceed. The truth is no amount of mental focus will help you solve every problem you'll face—or determine the right paths to take. Over thinking your choices and decisions will only create doubt and uncertainty and keep you from pursuing your dreams.

To avoid getting stuck, at times you'll have to look beyond the confines of your mind and simply trust your gut. Achieving success and happiness takes more than thinking—you must also trust your *feelings*. The hunches and impulses that you experience every day are how your genius often speaks to you.

It takes intellect and instinct to find your truth.

Following My Instincts

When I least expect it a distinct feeling comes over me—an intense feeling of excitement; a sudden surge of creativity; a strong sense of urgency. That's when I know that my genius wants to communicate with me. As soon as I feel it, if I can, I run to my computer to capture every idea and insight that is whirling around in my head. If I'm not at my computer, I jot down my thoughts in a notebook I keep with me at all times. Sometimes I find myself writing well past midnight because, for whatever reason, my genius prefers to come alive in the middle of the night.

Late one evening, a few months after I returned from my first coaching class, I couldn't fall asleep. After lying awake in bed for several hours, I suddenly began to sense that *feeling*. My instincts were telling me to get out of bed, turn on my computer, and write an e-mail message to my manager, Pat, about what had been on my mind for the past few weeks. I did as my inner guidance told me and I held nothing back.

I told Pat that I felt that with all of the recent organizational changes that had taken place, many people within HP had lost their spirit. I said that I wanted to help him create an energized and empowered organization that knew no limits. I shared with him my passion for coaching and employee development and wrote that I wanted to play a major role in boosting employee retention and building our organization's bench strength. The message was written straight from the heart—direct and unedited, expressing everything I honestly felt in that particular moment. I kept writing until I said everything that mattered to me and then I immediately pushed the send button. I knew that if I had hesitated at all, I would have chickened out and quickly caved in to my fears and doubts.

The following morning I anxiously waited for Pat's response. Every time I heard the Outlook e-mail chime I rushed to check for his reply. I didn't hear from him that day or the next day, and soon a week passed by. I'd speak to Pat on conference calls and see him in staff meetings, but he never mentioned the message. Looking back, I'm sure he must have been in shock. When I re-read the message the raw honesty I expressed even startled me.

After weeks of waiting, I finally found the courage to pull Pat aside in the hallway one afternoon to tell him why I felt compelled to write my midnight missive. "I know my message probably caught you by surprise," I said, "but please don't ignore me. I simply want to talk to you about how I can really bring value to your team." I was nervous about what he would say but thankfully, he responded favorably. He told me that he didn't have time to talk then, but he agreed to have a one-on-one with me the following week.

As we sat across from each other in his office, I spoke openly and passionately about my goals and vision. As I excitedly shared my thoughts and ideas, Pat leaned back comfortably in his chair and just listened.

After I finished talking, Pat said, "I can tell how much becoming a coach means to you." Before I could respond he said, "But are you any good at it?" Without hesitating, I emphatically said, "Yes!" Then we both had a good long laugh.

We continued to discuss my interests for awhile longer and then I noticed that the expression on Pat's face changed and he suddenly stopped talking. We sat there in silence for several seconds and I wondered, *"What is he thinking?"* Just as I was mustering up the courage to ask him, he started to share his *feelings*. He said that he really wanted to help me fulfill my dreams inside HP, but he admitted that he honestly didn't know what options would be available to me. He explained that he didn't know if my desires aligned with HP's priorities. Even though I was disappointed in his response, I appreciated his honesty and thought that would be the end of our discussion. Just as I was about to excuse myself, he unexpectedly said, "I have an idea. I don't know what I'll be able to do for you, but in the meantime, I think I could use some personal coaching to help me lead my new sales organization. If you're as good at it as you say you are, you can try out your new coaching skills on me."

I couldn't believe what I was hearing. My manager was willing to let me coach him. He must be kidding! He wasn't. And that's exactly how I got my first coaching client.

Because this was an unprecedented experience, Pat and I established clear boundaries for our partnership. During coaching sessions, Pat gave me full reign to help him address his business and leadership challenges. After each session ended,

I maintained confidentiality and went back to focusing on my sales and marketing responsibilities. Pat and I were committed to making this a win/win opportunity, and in the end, we both met our objectives. He felt more effective leading his sales team and I got one step closer to fulfilling my professional dreams. But this amazing experience never would have happened if I hadn't trusted my instincts after midnight one evening.

Fueled by that positive experience, I made a promise to myself that going forward I'd always follow my heart and trust myself. If something felt right, I'd pursue it regardless of the perceived risks. Nine months after I sent that e-mail message to Pat, I faced a test to see if I had the guts to keep that promise.

Delivering the Package

After I finished my coach training classes, I was beginning to sense that it was time to do something out of the ordinary. For weeks, I kept trying to figure out what to do, but nothing grabbed my interest. Then one morning, that feeling hit me again and this time it was very intense. My instincts were telling me that it was time to up the ante and share my ideas and beliefs with the highest ranking executive inside HP. I didn't understand "why," but I couldn't deny what I was feeling inside. I knew this action could lead to career suicide, but a promise is a promise, especially the ones we make to ourselves. So I accepted the risk and sent Mark Hurd, the CEO of HP, a package.

It was a simple and elegant wooden box. The words, *The Package*, were engraved on the glass opening on the lid of the box. Inside, I placed several personal items. They were random things that I thought revealed who I was and what I had achieved—past performance evaluations, a touching thank you card from a former employee, and even a before and after picture of my newly remodeled kitchen with a post-it note attached that said, "I can see possibilities." I carefully selected every item to reveal a personal part of me, the human side of a high-potential employee.

After I selected all of the items, I placed a personal letter on top of the contents so that it would be visible through the glass opening. I closed the box and drove to the nearest UPS store and paid $81.03 for next-day delivery.

On the following page is an excerpt from the letter I sent to Mark Hurd—totally unabashed and *unleashed*.

Stephanie Chick

April 21, 2005

Mark Hurd
Chief Executive Officer
Hewlett-Packard Company
3000 Hanover Street
Palo Alto, CA 94304-1112

Dear Mark:

Welcome to HP! I know that you've already received over 1,000 e-mails from HP employees. I hope that you can bear to read just one more letter, along with **"The Package"** that I've carefully selected for you. The contents of this package reflect one employee's accomplishments, dreams, challenges, lessons learned ... and potential. There are many more packages inside HP waiting to be opened.

I'd like to share a brief personal story with you. At the age of four, I experienced a very traumatic event. My reaction to the event was very unpredictable, yet it provided me with an important life lesson. I didn't cry. I didn't tell anyone. I didn't get angry. I simply went outside and rode my bike. I am now 42—a dynamic, accomplished, and charismatic African-American woman. Over the past two weeks, I have finally been able to release my childhood trauma and embrace my life's purpose. What a life-changing experience this has been for me! My unfortunate childhood experience taught me how to ride through the joys and turbulence of life while pursuing one's calling.

My life purpose is to *"Deliver the Package and help others deliver theirs."* The package represents my authenticity and the unmatched experience of knowing how to unleash individual purpose and potential. My professional goal is to help others deliver their packages and unleash their genius—to benefit our customers, shareholders, and employees. As we continue our company-wide transformation efforts, we must focus on personal transformation as well. I want to partner with you in helping HP harness the authentic power of its employees.

Mark, this package is for you only. I'm requesting a 30-minute meeting with you to discuss the contents of the package that I've sent and to see if we can explore a win/win partnership. I have set very aggressive personal, professional, and financial goals for myself over the next four years. I understand my purpose and potential and am ready to partner with you to create a high performance organization that capitalizes on the strengths of its employees. I will attempt to deliver the package three times. Afterwards, I will assume that I have reached the wrong address and I'll get back on my bike and continue riding to my next destination. If you decide not to accept this package, that's okay. We'll both continue on our own separate journeys. Again, welcome aboard and I look forward to hearing from you soon.

All the best,

Stephanie Chick

I still can't believe that I did that! The letter was filled with over-the-top bravado and it was a bit too personal. However, in the beginning stages of unleashing your genius, your actions might be somewhat unrefined and unwieldy. That's what can happen when you're desperate to be free.

I never received a reply from Mark Hurd—not that I really expected to. However, I've often wondered what happened to the package. Maybe it was intercepted by a staffer who immediately discarded it. Perhaps Mark received it but pushed it aside due to more pressing priorities. Or maybe he didn't respond because he thought I was an unbalanced employee in need of counseling. To be honest, finding out what happened to the package wasn't of much concern to me—then or now. What was really important to me was that I had found the courage to trust my instincts. I knew for sure that I had to deliver that package and once it was sent, I felt settled and content. I was at peace.

But that's not the end of the story ....

After I left HP, one of my first major coaching clients was Xerox, where I was hired to help coach and develop high-potential employees. Before meeting with my new coaching clients, I met with several senior leaders to explain my approach and philosophy. One of the senior leaders I met with was Ursula Burns, who was then the president, and was recently named Xerox's CEO. We had a very spirited discussion about employee development—what works and what doesn't. I also spoke about the rigorous coaching program I had planned and assured Ursula that the coaching experience would exceed her expectations. As I sat across from her, I spoke with confidence and certainty. I was completely comfortable and at ease talking about the value I could offer Xerox employees.

After fifteen or twenty minutes had passed, I sensed it was time to leave. So I stood up, shook Ursula's hand, and thanked her for meeting with me. That's when I suddenly recalled the package I had sent to Mark Hurd two years earlier. At the time, I didn't understand why I was so compelled to send the box and letter to him, but now it all made sense.

I realized that sending the package to Mark had been my dress rehearsal for this opportunity. It was a dry run to prepare me to stand up for my convictions, particularly with people who hold powerful positions. Although it was bold and risky to deliver a package to the CEO of HP, that experience gave me the confidence to share my ideas and beliefs with high ranking executives inside *any* Fortune 500 company. Your genius knows what lies ahead and if you listen closely and follow where it leads you, it will prepare you well in advance.

Always follow your hunches, creative impulses, and unexplained urges to do radical things. Even if you don't understand *why*, trust your instincts and be willing to go along for the ride. To deliver your package, you must follow your heart and stay open to whatever life has in store.

Genius chooses to explore what talent hastily ignores.

ALIGNMENT

As you take action, find people who can and want to help you achieve your dreams. Everyone needs a helping hand to succeed—Tiger had Earl, Oprah has Gayle, and of course, Barack needs Michelle. Surround yourself with people who are willing to share their knowledge, talents, and resources to help you maximize your abilities. Stay aligned with people who are invested in your success and happiness—inside and outside your company.

Over the years, many people have helped me deliver my package and I'm deeply grateful for their support and guidance. First and foremost, my loving husband who supports me unconditionally and has made tremendous sacrifices to allow me to set my genius free; a close circle of loyal friends who have nurtured my dreams as if they were their own; colleagues and mentors who have helped me learn and grow. There have also been countless people I've met only briefly, yet their comments, ideas, and suggestions have inspired and influenced me. In ways large and small, many people have played a role in helping me unleash my power and potential.

To deliver your package you need a support system, people who will champion your dreams and generously share their expertise and experiences to help you reach your goals. Don't try to deliver your package alone.

Learning to leverage the genius of
others helps you unleash your own.

I often counsel my clients on how to stay aligned with the supportive people who are invested in their success. They come into coaching sessions complaining about their strained personal and professional relationships. They're frustrated and stressed, feeling like they've completely run out of ideas about what to do next. If you've ever found yourself feeling the same way, the following delivery tips will help you maintain more positive and productive relationships with people who can and want to help you deliver your package.

Be Explicit About What You Need

I often find that my clients fail to clearly express their wants and needs. They dance around their true desires and expect other people to be mind readers. One client told me what she desired in terms of work/life balance, her next career move, and what she felt was getting in the way. She wanted to travel less for the next three months so she could spend time with her daughter before she headed off to college. And based on her performance and the positive feedback she received about her leadership skills, she felt that she would be ready to step into a VP position the next year. I asked her what happened when she discussed her desires with her boss and she said, "Well, I've told him some of my interests but I haven't been *this* specific." During our coaching conversation, I discovered that the reason why she was hesitant to ask for what she really wanted was because her company was going through another restructuring, and she was afraid that she'd get push back.

You won't find out what's possible for you to achieve inside your company, or anywhere else, if you don't find the courage to have "tough conversations" with people who can help you realize your dreams. Don't be afraid to be direct and honest with *anyone* about your wants and needs.

If you don't ask, you can't receive.

Relationships Are a Two-Way Street

Often, we get so focused on our own agenda—what *we* want and what *we* need, that we forget that others have yearnings, too. It isn't always about you. While you're trying to deliver your package, someone else is attempting to deliver theirs, too. Remember that relationships must be mutually rewarding. In successful partnerships, each person's needs, wants, and expectations have to be addressed to maintain harmony. You'll stay aligned with people at work and in life if you know when to give and how to receive.

When to Give

You'll know when to give by carefully listening and observing. We've all had the experience of working with someone on a project when suddenly something changes. You notice that the energy between the two of you has shifted—sometimes it's subtle, sometimes significant. Things were going along smoothly and then there's a slight tension, awkwardness, an unevenness of some kind. These are the signs that the relationship is out of alignment.

Several years ago, I worked with my colleague, Mark, on an initiative to increase our organization's sales performance. For over two years, we collaborated on a number of projects together. At times we had our differences of opinion on how to tackle business challenges, however, we always managed to stay aligned and had become good friends.

I was the lead on the sales initiative and proposed a strategy to help us reach our objectives. My sales team would implement a new process that allowed them to close inbound leads more quickly. Mark has keen analytical skills and wanted to help me assess another option that might be more effective. Instead of welcoming his perspectives, I continued to push forward with my plans. Mark tried several times to get me to consider his ideas but I refused to listen. I was certain that I had figured out the right strategy and I wanted to get things launched quickly. As a last resort, Mark called me to see if we could meet face-to-face to discuss our differences. Instead of talking about when we would meet, our conversation escalated into a heated argument and afterwards, we stopped speaking.

A few weeks before I was going to implement the leads process, I saw Mark at a team luncheon. It was very awkward and uncomfortable between us. We could hardly look each other in the eyes. As I sat there, I reflected on what transpired between us during the past few weeks. As I glimpsed at Mark out of the corner of my eye, I could tell that he was visibly shaken by what had happened. The look of pain and disappointment on his face moved me and that's when it hit me—the damage that I had done. This time the *feeling* was telling me that I needed to give Mark an apology.

In my e-mail message, I told Mark how much I regretted that I didn't sit down with him to discuss his suggestions. I asked for his forgiveness. I told him that if he was willing, I wanted to start over, and this time I would thoughtfully listen. Mark immediately replied and thanked me for reaching out. He accepted my apology and he also took the time to share a few of his thoughts and feelings. Mark said he wondered why I was driving so hard to implement a solution without getting input or *alignment*. He told me he felt hurt and disrespected by my actions. He didn't understand how a two-year relationship could get destroyed so quickly when he had always supported and believed in me.

I was so focused on what I wanted to achieve that I ignored Mark's feelings. I hadn't taken the time to give him what he needed, which in essence was my respect for his point of view. That's what really caused our feud.

You'll always know when it's time to give if you pay attention to the dynamics in your relationships. We often know when we've done something to upset the balance, but because we're overly focused on our own needs, we ignore other people's priorities. Relationships require give and take. You have to care about another person's challenges and objectives as much as you're concerned about what's on your plate. If you remember one thing, it will keep your relationships from coming unglued.

*It's time to give when you
realize it's been all about you.*

How to Receive

I learned how to receive from my mentor and friend, Marshall Goldsmith. Marshall is one of the nation's leading executive coaches and considered to be one of the top 50 business thinkers globally. He's worked with over a hundred major CEOs and his coaching insights have been featured in major publications such as *Business Week*, *Harvard Business Online*, and *Fast Company*.

Marshall has helped me publish several articles and counseled me on many occasions about my business plans. We both live in San Diego and I've enjoyed many long Saturday morning walks with him and his dog, Beau. Each time we're together, Marshall generously shares anything he thinks I need to know that would help me realize my potential.

I met Marshall a few months after I left HP when I contacted him for guidance as I launched my professional coaching practice. I felt overwhelmed after leaving behind the safety and security of the corporate world to run my own company. I had so many questions. There were many things I didn't understand about how to build my brand and develop a compelling value proposition for my clients. Now that I had taken the leap, I felt very uneasy about how to proceed. Thankfully, I quickly realized that one of the first things I needed to do was to find someone in my field to act as a mentor to me, someone who had already walked in my shoes and would be willing to share his or her learnings and success strategies. After reading several articles on his website, I had the feeling that Marshall was the one who could guide me on the next leg of my journey. So I wrote the following e-mail message to him—hoping and praying that he would respond to my plea.

Hi Marshall,

I am a genius coach in search of a genius coaching mentor. That's the bottomline. I'm also an African-American with big dreams and a unique, powerful voice. I know that I need to find mentors at the top who are willing to provide guidance and support… and who can recognize my genius. A big, bold request—but then again I've never played it safe. [not exactly true but in this instance it was]

I thank you in advance for considering my request. Please check out my website at www.deliverthepackage.com. My belief is that we all have a genius within—a package that eagerly waits to be opened.

I eagerly anticipate your call…

Stephanie

I didn't know if I'd ever hear from Marshall. I knew he was very busy and he traveled frequently. I figured it would be weeks before I received a response from him—if at all. But I was wrong. When I opened my e-mail the next morning, the following reply was waiting for me in my inbox.

Dear Stephanie,

Greetings from New York!
It is great to hear from you!
I will be happy to talk to you.
Please just call and schedule time for us to talk.
Courage is a good thing!
I liked your website.

Life is good.

Marshall

I was humbled by Marshall's kindness. I couldn't believe that a perfect stranger, and a well-known one at that, had taken the time to immediately respond to my inquiry. I knew that executives paid him hundreds of thousands of dollars for his expertise, yet he was willing to share his time with me for free.

I was deeply grateful for his generosity and immediately scheduled a phone call with him for the following week.

I could immediately sense that Marshall was the right mentor for me. He was very personable, direct, and had a great sense of humor. I felt he was genuine. We talked briefly about our personal and professional backgrounds and then Marshall began to offer his advice about the lessons he had learned, strategies that worked for him, and suggestions on what to do next. He came to the call prepared to freely give to me. However, instead of simply listening and learning, instead of knowing how to receive, I kept interrupting him with my thoughts and opinions. The third time I did this, Marshall verbally slapped me across the face by swiftly saying, **"Shut up!"**

I was stunned. A range of emotions—shock, surprise, embarrassment, and humiliation washed over me. In less than ten minutes I had somehow alienated this person I admired and had blown a great opportunity. I knew that I needed to make a quick decision about what to do next. I could get angry, let my ego tell him a thing or two, and then slam down the phone. Or I could humble myself and accept his tongue lashing. I chose to do the latter and that's when I received an invaluable lesson.

When Marshall told me to shut up, he wasn't being mean or rude. He needed to get my attention because I wasn't listening. Marshall told me that people seek help and then try to show how smart they are by challenging viewpoints and commenting on what someone has to say. It's funny how we can let our egos get out of control, causing us to do things that get us in our own way.

Marshall's feedback was hard to hear, but he was right. I was so concerned about impressing him with my knowledge that I forgot the purpose of our call… for me to receive *his* insights. The greatest lesson I learned from Marshall that day was when someone is ready to give to you, be grateful, and allow yourself to receive their gifts.

Every day you'll meet people who are eager and willing to help you deliver your package, but you have to be willing to accept their generosity. Recently, I offered to help a friend who had been laid off. She couldn't afford my coaching services so I offered to give her an hour of my time for free. I sat eagerly at my desk waiting for her call, but the phone didn't ring. I was ready to give, but she didn't show up to accept my generosity. A day later she wrote me an apologetic e-mail. She had gotten "busy" and forgot to put our appointment on the calendar. When someone makes the effort to help you, don't let your ego or your busy life block your blessings.

By learning when to give and how to receive you'll stay in harmony with people who want to help you set your genius free. That's how life and living is supposed to be.

When you stay aligned with the right people, you'll deliver your package with less effort and greater ease.

ASSESSMENT

As you take action, each day will bring new insights and discoveries and over time you'll figure out what it takes to set your genius free. The key to staying on track and making progress will be rigorous and consistent self-assessment. Every day you have to be willing to take a hard look in the mirror to assess what's working and what's preventing you from delivering your package. Sometimes when you look at your own reflection, you won't like what you see. Other times, you'll discover something remarkable and intriguing.

Genius is the by-product of continuous learning.

Ongoing learning is the key to setting your genius free. If you commit yourself to learning about who you are and where you're going every day, you'll continue to unleash your genius and achieve endless possibilities. In my coaching practice, I've consistently noticed that the key difference between the clients who succeed in delivering their package and those who don't is that those who maximize their abilities have an insatiable thirst for learning. Just remember that if you're courageous enough to keep learning from every step and misstep, you'll stay on the path to delivering your package.

I should caution you, though. Learning is just the first half of the equation. Once you learn your lessons you must then *apply* them. In other words, learning is of no use if you fail to incorporate what you've learned into future choices and decisions. Unfortunately, I've seen far too many people fail to take action on the things that they've learned and know to be true. Many people invest a great deal of time, energy, and money pursuing personal growth opportunities. They buy tons of self-help books, attend motivational conferences, and even invest in coaching. They do all the right things to learn and grow, yet for whatever reason the learning is never translated into anything tangible. The result—they never maximize their potential.

> *Applying lessons learned is a*
> ***must*** *for unleashing genius.*

The best way for me to keep track of lessons learned, so that I remember to apply them is to keep a learning journal. Each evening, after having dinner and spending time with my husband, I steal off to my favorite comfy chair in our family room with a cup of chamomile tea and honey, and a warm blanket on chilly evenings. That's when I slow down and get really quiet and still—taking time to reflect on what I learned throughout the day. I review my experiences and write down at least one key takeaway, something that I've learned that I can put into practice the following day. I've done this consistently for many years and each time I sit down I never find it hard to capture an important lesson.

> *Learning never ends.*

My Greatest Lesson Learned

I've learned so much during my journey to unleash my genius inside and outside corporate America. I've learned how to be both patient and persistent; I've learned how to trust myself; I've learned the importance of asking for help. I've learned so many things that have enabled me to set my genius free, and as a result, each day I feel genuinely happy and at peace.

If I had to pick the most significant lesson I've learned over the years about unleashing genius it is: **the power of choice**.

No matter what your circumstances are, you have the ability to make a choice about what you want for your life—both personally and professionally. You can decide if you want to leave your genius trapped or if you want to set it free. It doesn't matter what's happened in the past or how far you feel you're off track. At any moment in time, you can make the choice to unleash your genius and deliver your package. It's never too late.

Choice doesn't have an expiration date.

In his book *The 8th Habit*, author Stephen Covey talks about the power of choice. He writes about visiting a library and being drawn to a passage in a book that dramatically shifted his thinking. The passage was, "Between stimulus and response there is a space. In that space lies our freedom and power to choose..." When I read those words they had a profound effect on me, too.

Choice is the greatest asset that we possess—yet it's the package that's often left unopened. Choice requires change. Unfortunately, it's human nature to resist change of any kind. We crave comfort, predictability and security. The problem with that strategy is that you'll stay stuck and find yourself lulled into accepting a life of mediocrity and random success.

Without choice you leave your life to chance.

Deliver the Package isn't about being content, complacent, and a willing victim of life's circumstances. Delivering *your* package is about leading your life with clear intentions and making proactive, conscious choices that maximize your abilities. Making the choice to unleash your genius puts you in charge; it puts you in the driver's seat of your own life. If you dare to believe that you have unlimited power and potential, you can leave a lasting legacy.

Your possibilities are endless if you
make the choice to set your genius free.

Stephanie Chick

The Delivery Tips

I hope this book inspires you to take the first step toward setting your genius free. The five daily disciplines and the simple truths dispersed throughout this book will guide you on your journey. As you begin the process of unleashing your genius, remember three important things:

You have unlimited power and potential.

You can achieve great things if you
believe and act courageously.

You are worthy.

There's nothing I want more than for you to realize your full potential—at work and in life. I know what I achieved and how I felt every day before I began to unleash my genius—and how much my life has changed since I took the leap to set my genius free. I've been on both sides of the fence, and I know for sure that there is a profound difference. I want you to experience boundless professional and personal success, and the indescribable feeling of bliss that comes with delivering your true package.

I think it's important for you to understand what you're signing yourself up for before you embark on your journey to unleash your genius. I want to explain what I feel are a few key factors that will prepare you for the journey and increase your odds of succeeding with the Delivery Process. Here are a few tips to help you decide if you're *really* ready to deliver your package.

You Must Have Desire to Deliver

You must have a burning desire to discover your true power and potential. The desire to unleash your genius has to be more than a passing interest—you've got to really *want* it. If your desire is strong it will be reflected in your attitude and actions. There will be a fire in your belly and you'll be ready to pursue your passions and purpose with a vengeance.

When I meet potential clients, the first thing I try to discern is if they really want to unleash their genius. I know that if they don't really want it, they won't have the stamina and strength to go the distance. After I've begun working with clients, I continue to monitor their behavior to make sure they're driven and motivated. A few times, I've had to "fire" clients when it was clear that, for whatever reason, their desires had faded.

The truth is, you don't "have to" unleash your genius and deliver your package. You can make it through life without setting your genius free. If you utilize your God-given talents and work hard, you can have a successful career and provide for your family. If that's all you want out of life, there's nothing wrong with that. It just means that your desire isn't strong enough to *Deliver the Package*.

Before you make the choice to deliver your package, ask yourself two important questions: What package do I want to deliver? How bad do I want it? On a scale of one to ten, if your desire isn't at least an eight... wait!

The Journey Won't Be Easy

The journey to unleashing your genius is incredibly fulfilling and rewarding, but the truth is, and many people don't want to hear this, it takes work. Tapping into your hidden creativity and capabilities takes never-ending dedication and *discipline*. The rewards are worth it, but to reap them, you'll have to make a life-long commitment.

Like life, the path to delivering your package is not always direct. It can be unpredictable; often taking unexpected twists and turns. The playground of genius is filled with curiosity, exploration, and discovery. If you're used to rigid planning and being in control of everything, unleashing your genius might make you feel uneasy. Just remember that being able to stay open and loose is what it means to live *free*.

The journey to unleash your genius will bring triumphs and trials, successes and failures, joy and pain. You'll experience ups and downs, and everything in between, if you make the choice to set your genius free. Think about Steve Jobs' journey. He was forced out of the company he co-founded, only to be brought back as CEO twelve years later. Since returning, he has helped his company develop breakthrough technologies that have transformed the music and mobile device industries. But he also had to fight cancer and deal with other serious health problems while creating one of the most innovative and influential companies in the world.

For all of us, the journey to unleashing our genius will be filled with magic, messiness, and mystery. Through it all, you just have to keep delivering...

Recently, I received a few unexpected e-mails from former clients sharing what they learned from their "genius" journeys. One client said, "Focusing on my real goals and facing my fears HAS NOT BEEN EASY... but that's not what I asked for." Another client wrote, "Despite our very hard work, I would not have changed any of it. I got sick of it, at times, but I needed it and feel more solid in my core than I have ever felt. That is a very good feeling."

Unleashing your genius will be challenging and rigorous, but the rewards are well worth it.

Love is the Key

To succeed at delivering your package, the most important advice I can give you is to follow your heart. Mozart said, "Neither a lofty degree of intelligence nor imagination nor both together go to the making of genius. Love, love, love, that is the soul of genius." Essentially, love is the key to setting your genius free.

Unleashing your genius requires that you love yourself, pursue work that you love, and establish loving and mutually supportive relationships with people who can help you maximize your abilities.

Believe it or not, love and business can co-exist. In fact, love has always existed inside companies; it's just been there under the guise of less threatening terminology: *passionate, creative, inspiring*. When these words are used to describe people, what it really means is that the person loves what they're doing.

In his book, *Think BIG and Kick Ass*, Donald Trump talks about his desire to do work that he truly loves. He states, "I don't have a burning desire to make money. I have a burning desire to enjoy what I do. It's never a money thing. I love building buildings, I love doing real estate, I love doing *The Apprentice*. I love doing the things that I do."

When your genius is unleashed, the feeling of *love* radiates through your work and your attitude.

Many employees feel that they can't discuss matters of the heart inside the workplace because it's not safe. They feel that if they expose who they really are and what's most important, it could possibly be used against them by colleagues or management. This may or may not be true. But ultimately, it's your life, and if you want to set your genius free, you must honor what makes your heart happy.

Love is the force that will keep you focused on unleashing your power and potential, no matter what obstacles or challenges you face. When you let love direct your choices and actions, you will stay on your path. You will *Deliver the Package*.

Deliver the Package

Acknowledgments

First and foremost, I give thanks to God for blessing me with such a powerful calling and purpose. Deliver the Package is Your will, not mine. In everything I do, I give You the glory.

To family members, friends, colleagues, and clients, thank you for inspiring me, and for your encouragement and well wishes. Each of you has left a lasting imprint on my heart and in my life.

To Laurie Hacking, Ashaki Rucker, Heather Shepard, and Linda Williams, you've kept me motivated and have always been there with open arms whenever I called. Your steadfast love and support have sustained me during my journey to complete this book. I'm deeply grateful for your "above the call of duty" generosity.

To my writing partner and creative muse, Kellie Tabron, without a doubt, this book would not have been completed without your dedication and guidance. You helped me search my soul and faithfully stayed by my side during the highs and lows. Your patience, kind and loving spirit, and ingenious insights helped me deliver this important package. Thank you for nurturing my hopes and dreams as if they were your own.

To my parents, Doris and Walter Youngblood, thank you for playing a major role in shaping who I am. Thank you for patiently listening to my endless ideas and plans, for being my biggest fans, and for teaching me how to give generously and unconditionally. To my father, James Willis, thank you for always telling me how much you love me and for teaching me how to be a strong and confident entrepreneur.

To my son, Eric, my love for you is the driving force behind everything I do. I've learned far more from you than you have from me. You're the one who showed me how to live free.

To my husband, Don, words can't adequately express how lucky and blessed I am to have you in my life. You are my best friend and my number one delivery partner. It's because of you that I am able to follow my dreams and fulfill my destiny. I can't ever repay you for what you've done for me. You are my soul mate and I love you dearly.

To Gigi, you have gone home to glory, but the warmth of your love is with me every day. Thank you for lighting the way...

About the Author

Stephanie Chick is the visionary creator of Deliver the Package®, a breakthrough coaching model that teaches you how to unleash your personal genius—in the workplace and beyond. Prior to launching Deliver the Package®, Stephanie worked in corporate America for over fifteen years at IBM and HP in sales, business development, and marketing.

Stephanie's coaching insights have been featured in *BusinessWeek*, *Black Enterprise*, *Essence*, *Harvard Business Online*, and *Diversity, Inc.* Her coaching clients include corporate executives at major companies such as Xerox, Pepsi, HP, American Express, AT Kearney, Deutsche Bank, and Intel.

Stephanie resides in San Diego, CA with her husband, Donald, and her son, Eric.

To learn more about Deliver the Package, visit
www.deliverthepackage.com
or email Stephanie at
stephanie@deliverthepackage.com

Life is short.

Talent isn't enough.

Focus on the five disciplines to set your genius free.

6156554R0

Made in the USA
Charleston, SC
20 September 2010